Red Eggs and Dragon Boats

Celebrating Chinese Festivals

Carol Stepanchuk

Pacific View Press

Berkeley, California

To Sarah and Gregory

The following people have generously contributed their time and help in the making of this book: Sue Gartley, Folk Art International Resources for Education; Bob Lew, creative food consultant; Linda Janklow, San Francisco Craft and Folk Art Museum.

To my husband Bob, thank you for your patience, support, and kitchen expertise; and to publishers, Nancy Ippolito, Pam Zumwalt, and Bob Schildgen, their editorial know-how and suggestions were invaluable. Lastly, my appreciation to Mark Ong for his creative design skill and to Barbara Chan for selected drawings.

Selected recipes in this book were adapted from *In the Chinese Kitchen* by Shirley Fong-Torres, Pacific View Press, Berkeley, 1993, and *San Francisco Chinatown: A Walking Tour* by Shirley Fong-Torres, Pacific View Press, Berkeley, 1991.

Cover and text design by Mark Ong
Illustrations on pages 18, 26, 30, 37, 46 by Barbara J. Chan

Chinese calligraphy by Mr. Chow Sik-Kwan

List of illustrations

Copyright ©1994 by Carol Stepanchuk

Library of Congress Catalog Card Number: LC 93-85733
ISBN 1-881896-08-0

Printed in Hong Kong

2

Contents

Bright, funny costumes, parades, drums and gongs, good things to eat, excitement, joining together with family and friends—the festival spirit is familiar the world over.

Celebrating Chinese Festivals

Beginning: The Chinese word for beginning is **shi**. This is where to start—the excitement of something new.

This is a book about celebration. In China there are festivals, ceremonies, and celebrations every month of the year. Whenever you need a holiday, there's always one in sight. The New Year, the most exciting of them all, starts on the first day of the first lunar month (sometime between late January and early February according to the Western calendar). It is a movable celebration because, like most Chinese festivals, it's an event based on the lunar calendar. This way of keeping track of time is based on the cycle of the moon, and has been used for over 2,000 years. There are 12 months, of 29 or 30 days each. A lunar month starts on the new moon. Each New Year begins on the second new moon after the winter solstice (December 21), the shortest day of the year.

Some festivals such as the Mid-Autumn Moon Festival celebrate the seasons. Others, like the Dragon Boat Festival celebrate something that happened, or might have happened long ago. There is also a festival to honor family ancestors, the people who have come before us. This one, Clear Brightness, is one of the few that has a fixed date according to the sun calendar. And, lastly, to celebrate the cycle of family life, new babies are honored on the 30th day after their birth with a red egg and ginger party.

China is a big country, with big differences in climate, geography, and food. People of the South have somewhat different holiday customs than people in the North. They also make different treats and special foods. For New Year's, northerners make *jiao zi* (steamed dumplings filled with meat and vegetables, a cold-weather favorite). Southerners make sweets of warm-climate coconuts and peanuts. And during the Moon Festival, northerners make "mooncakes" with fillings of brown date paste or white sugar paste. In the South, the fillings include everything from ham and dates to walnuts and watermelon seeds.

China is well known for its differences in food, and every region has its own highlights. There are wheat and cabbages from Beijing, crab and fish from Shanghai, red peppers from Hunan, bamboo shoots and chilies from Sichuan, and rice and vegetables from the Yangzi river valley. The land is different too. There are dry, grass-covered steppes in the north, rolling hills in the south, the harsh Gobi desert in outer China, and the highest mountain in the world—Mt. Qomolangma (Everest)—in the southwest.

Chinese people also speak different versions or dialects of the Chinese language. The national language is the language of the north, called *putonghua* ("common speech"), or Mandarin, or *guoyu* ("national language") on Taiwan. People in the south (and many Chinese people in the United States and Canada) speak the Cantonese dialect. However, they all write their language the same way, using signs called "characters" to represent words, instead of an alphabet. Some characters look like the words they mean and are called "pictographs"; others show an idea and are called "ideographs."

And all Chinese have heard the same legends and stories of their holidays, too. They know about Qu Yuan, the first great poet of China, honored during the Dragon Boat Festival, and Chang E, the Moon Goddess, to whom everyone sends their wishes during the Moon Festival.

With this book you can join in the celebration of four big festivals, and a party for a baby. You'll discover some of the favorite ingredients of Chinese celebrations—from mooncakes and dragon boat dumplings to lantern riddles and sand-swallow kites. You'll also find words written in Chinese. To show how the words sound in Mandarin Chinese, we have written them here using our alphabet. When pronounced in Chinese, x sounds like sh—(shoe), c sounds like ts—(bats), and q sounds like ch—(chew). For example, *qun* is "chwun" and *cai* is "tsai."

Through the seasons and festivals of the Chinese calendar, you'll go full cycle—a cycle that stands not only for a full year, but for the fullness of family and the world around you. Remember, the spirit of celebration is a part of us all. Take it with you wherever you go!

The drummers lead off the Lantern Parade in this North China village.

Chinese Lunar New Year

Spring: Pronounced **chun,** spring is the season of beginnings.

Happy New Year! The New Year is the most exciting and colorful time of the year. Inside Chinese houses everywhere, you'll find dishes of oranges and apples for good luck, blossoming flowers for beauty, and hot plates of crab and fresh fish for great plenty. Everyone thinks only the best thoughts and everything looks clean and new. On New Year's Day, Day 1 of the New Moon, firecrackers are set off from morning until night. Dressed in new clothes and bringing gifts of oranges and tangerines, families visit friends and relatives. They eat bowls of noodles for long life. They munch on sugared melon which symbolizes good health, or on lotus seeds because the word for lotus (*lian zi*) sounds like the word for "lots of children." People shout the New Year greeting **GONG XI FA CAI (Happiness and Fortune to You).** During the New Year festivities, which begin at the close of the old year and last for about two weeks, close friends, cousins, aunts, and uncles gather together

to wish each other good luck,

to pay respects to their grandparents ten times back,

to send off the Kitchen God, and

to imagine what the zodiac animal in charge has in store for the coming year.

This is the time to say good-bye to the old year. Families get together for a New Year's Eve banquet. The last course eaten is fish because the word for fish in Chinese (**yu**) sounds like the word for "great plenty." The adults give all the children bright red "lucky money" envelopes with money inside. Mothers and fathers paste short poems called "spring couplets" on the doorways and gates of the house to welcome the New Year. These couplets are written on red paper because the color red means good luck. Everyone stays awake as long as they can playing games, telling stories, and making wishes to see the old year out.

The Kitchen God

A week before the New Year begins, the Kitchen God rides up through the sky to the palace of the Jade Emperor to make his report on the good and bad deeds of all families. There are many different legends about the Kitchen God. But all the stories agree about one thing— that ever since he left the Earth and was made Master of the Household by the Jade Emperor, the Kitchen God has brought only luck and happiness to all those who believe in him.

Long ago there was a carpenter named Zhang. He lived with his wife, Meiling, in a small house on a mountainside. Even though they had little money and few possessions, they were happy together. Their house always looked cheerful at New Year's when Meiling hung up lanterns in the courtyard and bright red couplets on either side of the front door.

But the winters were long and cold. Zhang and Meiling ate the rice they had stored away at springtime and tried to stay warm with their soft, cotton-padded quilts. Alas, one winter day, all the grain was gone. Sad to say, good fortune never came to their door. With no hope in sight, Zhang had to part from Meiling and marry her off to someone else. The carpenter now lived by himself in the tiny cottage.

Poor Zhang!

One day, Zhang was hired to work at a well-off family's house. He did not realize that this was Meiling's new home. Zhang repaired many things that day, and although he did not see Meiling, she knew who he was. Meiling still loved Zhang, but realized that he was still very poor. His clothes looked old and his boots were worn. She wanted to help in some way. Knowing he was proud and not likely to accept any gifts, she hid some gold coins in the sweet cakes that her maid packed for his journey home.

Offerings of sweets are placed out for the Kitchen God's long journey. Later, his picture is burned so the smoke will carry his spirit to the sky.

11

Spring Couplet

A two-line poem written in Chinese characters on red paper. The words describe good wishes and thoughts about the coming year. The first line of the poem is called the "head." The second line is called the "tail," and both phrases are paired with each other word for word. This one says:

"Hearing firecrackers far away,
  you'll know the year is new,
Seeing plum blossoms by
  chance, you'll know that
  Spring's here too."

On the way back to his cottage, Zhang stopped at a small teahouse for a rest. A traveler came up to him and offered a few pennies for one of his cakes. Zhang had not had a chance to eat any of the cakes and did not know about the treasures inside. He accepted the money and gave one cake to the traveler. The traveler said, "How good it tastes. The filling is so sweet. May I have another?" And so it went. The traveler ate three, four, five, six, seven cakes and though his stomach was quite full, he finished the whole basket. Of course, he pocketed the gold coins without saying a word to Zhang, and he went on his way.

Poor Zhang!

News of the unlucky carpenter spread throughout the universe. One day, the Jade Emperor came to Zhang and said, "You are a good and honest man, even though you have not had much luck. I shall, however, reward you with a noble position in the afterworld. I'll put you in charge of taking care of families because you have built and repaired so many kitchens and houses in your lifetime. I'll send for your wife who lived happily with you in your small house a long time ago. You can sit together over the stoves of families large and small, rich and poor, with lots of children and with few, and keep track of their good deeds and bad deeds."

Zhang agreed, and the Jade Emperor presented him with:

a set of new clothes;

two young helpers to hold the tallies of every good and bad deed;

a dog and a rooster;

a horse that could gallop to Heaven, and

a treasure urn filled with gold coins.

Lucky Zhang!

When the Jade Emperor had given the carpenter everything he needed to fulfill his role in office, he said, "A week before each Lunar New Year you must come and report to me about every family in the land. If you do this well and are fair, you will have a welcome spot in the heart of all homes and will never be without food, clothing, or money again."

And so it is, every year on the 23rd or 24th days of the 12th lunar month, the Kitchen God dutifully makes his report. At this time, families prepare special offerings of sweet cakes and sticky rice for him so that he will say only sweet things or, perhaps, his mouth will be so glued together he won't be able to say anything at all!

Sticky Rice

Also called glutinous rice, it is grown on dry ground (rice grown in wet paddy fields is what we're more used to eating). When it's cooked, it turns into a sticky, starchy mass that's very filling and fun to eat. The flour which comes from glutinous rice is used in making all kinds of desserts or as a thickener instead of corn starch.

Zodiac

The Chinese zodiac is divided into 12 parts and is used as a 12-year calendar. Each year is ruled by one of 12 animals. Five cycles of 12 years make up one complete cycle of 60 years—the basis of the Chinese calendar. When someone turns 60, and completes a full cycle, the family plans a big birthday celebration.

The zodiac cycle starts with the Rat, followed by the Ox, Tiger, Rabbit, Dragon, Snake, Horse, Sheep, Monkey, Rooster, Dog, and Pig. Lots of stories tell why the zodiac starts with the rat. One tells about the animals crossing a big river. The rat rode on the ox's back and jumped off at just the right time, winning the race. The ox came in second, and just as you might have thought, the pig came in last, because he never rushes.

Traditionally, when a child was born, fortune-tellers took careful note of the year of birth as well as the hour, day, and month to figure out the baby's destiny. According to Chinese folklore, every person has personality traits that are the same as their animal birth sign. What sign were you born under? What are you like? What will you become?

Rat—(1984, 1996) You are charming, well organized, logical, and careful not to waste a penny of your allowance. You will make a good architect, salesperson, or campaign manager.

Ox—(1985, 1997) Patient, determined, and easy going, you never miss a beat. You will be happy as a tennis pro, surgeon, hair stylist, or rock climber.

Tiger—(1986, 1998) You are brave, kind, daring, and full of feeling. You might be a race car driver, animal trainer, reporter, or soap opera star.

Rabbit—(1987, 1999) Rabbits are selfless, neat and tidy, and get along well with their brothers and sisters. You are well suited as a banker, lawyer, interior designer, or video-game player.

Dragon—(1988, 2000) One of the most showy characters in the zodiac chart, you are imaginative, lucky, full of fun, and energetic. You will make a good talk-show host, artist, or diplomat.

Snake—(1989, 2001) Yin to the dragon's yang, you are mysterious, quiet, and a deep thinker, successful as a philosopher, fortune-teller, or best friend.

Horse—(1978, 1990) You are cheerful, talkative, a hard worker, and a bit of a show-off. You will be best as an explorer, writer, or debutante.

Sheep—(1979, 1991) You're a strong believer in what you do, gentle and loving, and very talented in the arts. You will make a good author, therapist, or landscape architect.

Monkey—(1980, 1992) Very smart, you have a lot of wonderful ideas but are full of mischief. You will be good at everything you do, from famous magician to head of state.

Rooster—(1993, 2005) You are neat as a pin, have lots of confidence, and would like everything to be perfect. You will be happiest as a fashion model, actor, or world traveler.

Dog—(1982, 1994) Keeping an eye on everything, you are alert and dependable. You will be an excellent secret agent, psychiatrist, or librarian.

Pig—(1983, 1995) You are happy, good-natured, outspoken, but a little too trusting. You might do well as a craftsperson, art collector, or comedian.

Lantern Festival

All over China, lanterns made from wood, bamboo, silk, paper, and even sesame seeds are carried through the streets on the Lantern Festival (Day 15 of the New Year). Folklore says that the soft glowing lights of the lanterns help guide wandering ghosts home. Later, everyone watches for the 100-foot long paper and silk dragon to come out of hibernation. The dragon means strength and goodness, and in the New Year dance, it chases after the sun ball, the source of its power. Lanterns come in all shapes and sizes. Some look like fantastic crabs with moving claws or birds with wings that flap. There are lanterns called "pacing horses" which spin when they are heated from the flame of the candle or an electric bulb. There are lanterns as large as houses. In North China, where winters are cold, lanterns are even carved from blocks of river ice. Children make lanterns at school and hang riddles on them. Here is one.

"When drawn it is round, but when written it is square;
In cold weather it is short, and in hot weather long."

(Answer: "sun" or "day," *ri*)

(Since many Chinese characters look like pictures, it helps to make up riddles like this to remember how to write them.)

Lantern exhibitions and markets are a part of the New Year season, and even if you are not buying one, it's fun to go and look.

17

About Chinese Cooking

Wok

Every Chinese kitchen has one—a large metal pan with a curved bottom. Restaurants have been serving quickly prepared wok meals for over 1,000 years. The curved shape of the wok makes it easy to concentrate the heat, cooking food quickly and saving on fuel, always scarce in China. Woks are used for stir-frying, deep-frying, stewing, or steaming. You can pop popcorn in a wok too.

Steaming

A cooking method used since ancient times, steaming makes food especially delicate and full of flavor. To steam dumplings, set them on a rack. Rest the rack on top of a pan or wok filled with water and cover with a lid. Turn the stove onto high heat. The boiling water should never reach the food—instead the steam should circulate around the food and cook it. If you don't have a steamer rack, try an aluminum pie tin with lots of holes set on top of a small tuna can with the top and bottom punched out. You can also use your mother's collapsible metal steamer basket.

Festive Sweet Turnovers

During the New Year, everyone is busy in the kitchen preparing holiday treats for guests coming to the house and for visits to other people's homes. Sharing food brings people together. Sweet turnovers are New Year's favorites because it's traditional to start the year with something sweet.

Ingredients & Utensils

mixing bowl and dish
mixing spoon
measuring cups and spoons
wok or skillet
frying thermometer
small strainer with handle
large plate, covered with several paper towels

For the filling

1/2 cup shredded coconut
3/4 cup roasted peanuts
1/4 cup white sugar
1/4 cup brown sugar
1 tablespoon sesame seeds
1 egg
1 pound won ton skins
(flat sheets of noodle dough (about 3 inches square) made from flour and eggs—usually in the refrigerated or frozen food sections of most supermarkets)

For the frying

3 cups vegetable oil for deep frying

Step by Step

Make sure a grown-up has looked over the recipe and can help with the chopping and deep-frying.

❖ Gather all ingredients and tools.
❖ Chop the peanuts in a food processor, grinder, or blender. Put in a medium-size bowl and add the coconut, white and brown sugar, and toasted sesame seeds. Mix well.
❖ Use a fork to beat one egg. Set aside. Scoop a teaspoon of filling in the center of separate won ton skins. Fold each skin into a triangle. Dip your finger into egg and wet along the short edge, fold each edge over about 1/2 inch and press to seal.
❖ Fill a wok or deep frying pan with 3 cups of cooking oil. Have the grown-up heat the oil to 350–375 degrees. Carefully drop a few pieces in at a time and fry until golden brown (usually less than a minute). Take the turnovers out with the wire strainer and place on the dish. Now the fun part—sprinkle with sugar, let them cool for a moment, and serve. (Makes a batch of about 40).

Bringing gifts of food for the ancestors helps everyone learn about and remember their family's history.

Clear Brightness Festival

On the day of the Clear Brightness Festival (April 4, 5, or 6), children and their families get ready to honor their great-grandparents, their parents' parents, their own parents, and their relatives as far back as they can remember.

Everyone in the family goes together to the graves of their ancestors to sweep the stones and clear the weeds. Little pieces of red paper that look just like roof tiles are pasted on top of the tombstone. Then, food offerings of dumplings and oranges, meats and vegetables, cakes and candies are set out for the ancestors. It's fun to arrange the bowls, plates, cups, spoons, and chopsticks. Everything is organized just like a real meal because ancestors are believed to live in an afterworld that's like the world of the living. After these honored guests have enjoyed their meal, the real food is shared with family and friends who may have come a long way to take part in the get-together. In fact, the day is really like a holiday picnic, but with extra special meaning, because it's all about remembering who came before you, and realizing who you are and who your children will be.

Clear Brightness: Clear brightness is called **qing ming**—when the outside air and light becomes pure and clear as in springtime.

21

After the food is eaten, everyone relaxes and closes their eyes for a moment. It's time to think back about favorite relatives—the summer vacations spent at *yeye's* (father's father) house or when *taipopo* (great-grandmother on the father's side) put the babies to sleep in her lap by telling them fairy tales, folk tales, and riddles. It's a day for enjoying the warm spring weather and seeing how everyone in the family is connected, from generation to generation, forever and ever.

100 Family Names

The family name is very important. It carries the memory of ancestors from many generations ago. Family names in China are tied to certain places. In many Chinese villages most people have the same family name. Almost everyone can tell you where they fall in the line of descent from the founder of their village. Some people can even go back 30 or 40 generations, some even back to Confucius, 2,500 years ago!

In old China babies were given a special "lock necklace" with the Chinese words for "100 families." This necklace would "lock" the baby to the help and protection of 100 households. The network of families comes in handy for people who have started a new home overseas. For newcomers to a new land, people with the same family name are willing to lend a helping hand. And those back home will give their support as well. The sense of family is very strong even if family members are separated by thousands of miles. Everyone tries to stay in touch with their part of the family living in China and the part of the family living in the United States or Canada through New Year visits and birthday greetings and by offering whatever special help and arrangements they can.

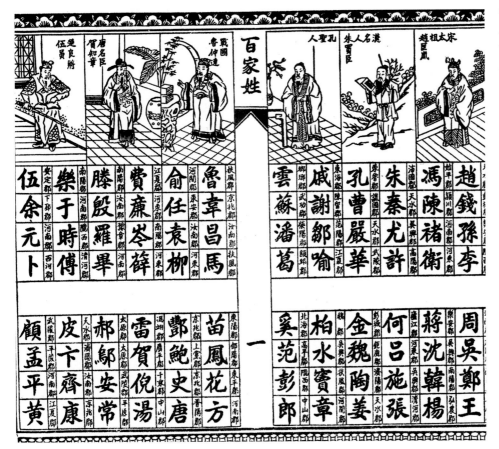

This is a page from the Chinese almanac and shows a listing of family names. The phrase "100 families" means the whole people—this section actually has over 500 surnames. The most famous ancestor of each family is pictured on top. The description below tells the name of the person and where the family originally came from.

Knowing your family history, generation after generation, can be very interesting. If we were to trace our families all the way back, we would find out that everyone is linked together in some way. In fact, if you think about it, we're all part of the same human family.

Flights of Fancy

The Clear Brightness Festival is a time to honor ancestors. It's also a time to picnic and play. A favorite pastime is flying kites. This time of year the winds are always favorable, and you can see kites in all kinds of shapes and designs in the sky. There are kites that look like

tadpoles,

frogs,

bats,

crabs,

cicadas,

butterflies,

heroes,

centipedes,

herons, and

dragonflies.

There's even a sand-swallow kite that flies in seven layers and a dragon kite so small that it can fit into your pants pocket.

Kites have been flown for thousands of years in China. Armies first used them to send messages. Later children and grown-ups began to fly them for pleasure especially during winter and springtime festivals. If the kite happened to disappear, it meant that bad luck and trouble disappeared too!

Today in China, the festival of Clear Brightness is still an occasion for flying kites of all varieties.

At the Chinese Table

Chopsticks

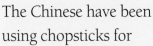

The Chinese have been using chopsticks for over 3,000 years. They use them for eating and cooking. In the beginning, it's easier to hold the sticks closer to the bottom, nearer the tips. As you get more used to them, you'll find you'll be holding them higher up. When you're really good, you'll be able to pick up peanuts, mushroom slices, and the penny that fell down next to your chair.

Tea

Tea is the traditional drink of China. One legend has it that the first tea plants sprang up where Bodhidarma, the 6th century Indian monk who brought Zen Buddhism to China, cut off his eyelids so that he could stay awake while meditating. However, tea was actually harvested, processed, and drunk as a daily beverage in China at least 800 years earlier.

Today China produces three major varieties of tea—green, black, and oolong—but all come from the same plant, *camellia sinensis,* a relative of the familiar flowering camellia. The small bushes grow best in mountainous areas. In the spring and summer the new leaves are picked by hand.

To produce tea the leaves are very carefully dried over heat while being stirred. Green tea is the favorite of most Chinese, who also like it when fragrant jasmine flowers are added. If the leaves are bruised by rolling them lightly, and allowed to stand a while before drying, they will darken and their flavor will change. Drying them when they are quite dark produces black tea. Most black tea is sold to other tea-loving countries. Drying the leaves when they are only partially dark produces oolong tea, with yet another flavor. This tea is popular in south China, where it is often served in tea houses in tiny clay pots.

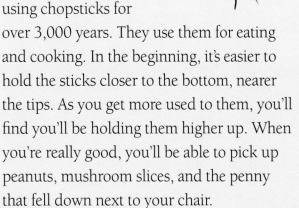

Almond & Sesame Cookies

This is a popular and easy-to-make treat that's perfect to take along on picnics. If you can't finish the whole batch in one day, they'll store well and taste just as good the next day.

Ingredients & Utensils

mixing bowls
mixing spoons, electric or hand mixer
measuring cups and spoons
sifter
pastry brush
cookie sheet
spatula
cooling rack

For the dough
2 1/2 cups flour
3/4 teaspoon baking soda
1 cup shortening, lard, margarine, or butter
1 cup sugar
1 egg
1 teaspoon almond extract
1/2 cup sesame seeds
1 cup crushed roasted almond
72 whole almonds

For the glaze
1 egg

Step by Step

Make sure a grown-up has looked over the recipe and can help with the baking.

❖ Gather all ingredients and tools.
❖ Preheat oven to 350 degrees. Lightly grease a cookie sheet. Put the sesame seeds in a small dish and set aside. Place the whole almonds nearby.
❖ Sift flour and soda into the mixing bowl. In another bowl, use mixer to combine shortening and sugar until fluffy. Then, gradually stir in the sifted flour and soda. Next, throw in the *crushed* almonds. Stir.
❖ Add egg and almond extract to this and mix. Roll the dough into golf-ball-size balls and dip into sesame seeds. Then, squash the balls to 1/2" thickness. Place one *whole* almond in the middle of each cookie. Put the cookies on the cookie sheet. Beat the other egg with a fork in a small bowl. Using the pastry brush, brush tops of cookies with the beaten egg for the glaze. Put in oven and bake for 15 minutes or until they've turned light brown. Carefully take them out of the oven and remove from cookie sheet with the spatula. Let them cool. (Makes 72 yummy cookies).

Guests bring new clothes, toys, and red envelopes with money as gifts for the new baby.

Full-Month Red Egg and Ginger Party

Full: The Chinese word **man** means fullness and plenty, the wholeness of new things.

Everything about babies is fresh, new and soft. Happy beginnings are celebrated with full-month red egg and ginger parties. When a new baby is a month old it is named and welcomed into the family. The Chinese wait a full month because in the past many new babies used to fall sick and die. So, until the baby had lived a full month, it wasn't really thought of as part of the family.

For the celebration, neighbors help new mothers by dying hard-boiled eggs red to give to relatives and friends. Special red lucky-money paper is boiled to make a red dye. As in weddings or festivals, the color red is used because it means happiness and good luck. Next, the women prepare ginger chicken soup with wine and tree ears (a kind of fungus that grows on the trunks of trees and adds a crunchy, wiggly texture to soups and vegetarian dishes). Ginger is important because in the *yin* (cold) *yang* (warm) balance of Chinese food, ginger adds a touch of "hotness" to the nutritional needs of the new mother, who is tired and weak (or too yin) after giving birth.

Tiger Clothes

Babies are given tiger hats, tiger shoes, and tiger bibs on their one-month birthday. In Chinese folklore, the tiger is the king of beasts and is believed to have special powers for protecting children. Babies have their hair cut on this day, too. The tiger hat that covers their heads has gold, silver and jade charms sewn on it for good luck. The tiger shoes have embroidered eyes that are sewn wide-open. These open eyes on their feet help keep children from tripping as they first learn to walk!

The celebration dinner for the guests can happen at home or in a restaurant. Everyone gives the baby new clothes, toys, and red envelopes filled with money. In the past, these parties were only given for boy babies, but nowadays girls are celebrated too. Everyone has fun honoring the one-month baby. Here's a new face to welcome into a changing world.

26 Unlucky Gates

ONE... TWO... THREE...

There's a lizard man chasing me!

As children grow older, they need more than tiger hats to protect them from danger.

Chinese children are told about a lizard man who carries a stick and has a funny-shaped head. He pesters children and hides

near gates,

around bridges,

next to cradles,

close to fire,

beside the bath,

on bolts of lightening.

He's everywhere, and no one likes him the least little bit. Depending on your birthdate or which of the Five Elements (earth, wind, water, fire, metal) are in your horoscope, your mother tells you which "26 gates" or "troubles" to avoid—like running after dogs or crossing bridges and streets. Because you never know where or when the monster man will appear and cause an accident.

Mean old monster.

There's only one danger that fits your birthdate, but mothers worry about them all. There's no way to escape him, until you grow up. Then he disappears forever.

I know it's silly,
but, one . . . two . . . three . . .
he's still after me!

Zhong Kui

Another way to protect against accidents is to hang pictures of the ghost-eater Zhong Kui. Zhong Kui was a great scholar, but he was so ugly that he was never given a special title or rank. The Emperor, feeling sorry about this, decided to honor him in the afterworld. Zhong Kui became so happy that he promised the Emperor in a dream that he would never let any ghosts or demons run free. Legends say Zhong Kui can catch any kind of troublemaker and stamp out all signs of trouble with his big black boots.

Game of Destiny

On a baby's first birthday, the parents lay out writing brushes, an abacus, scissors, ruler, scale, and other things. Whatever the baby grabs or likes to hold tells what the baby might become when he or she grows up. The brushes would mean a teacher, an abacus and scale would mean a store manager, the scissors would mean a craftsperson, the ruler would mean a carpenter. Today parents add toy cars and calculators.

God of Long Life

A popular decoration at birthday parties is the God of Long Life. He's usually pictured holding the Peach of Immortality. Legend says that the best peaches are found in the Garden of the Queen Mother of the West and ripen every 3,000 years. If you're lucky enough to eat one, you can live forever. If not, a bowl of long life noodles is at least a start.

Happy Birthday Long Life Noodles

This a special Beijing noodle dish served on birthdays. Eating a bowl of long, extra-thin noodles on your birthday means you'll live a long and happy life. Just remember not to break any of the noodles while eating!

Ingredients & Utensils

cooking pot
strainer
bowl
knife and cutting board
wok or skillet
1 pound thin fresh Chinese-style thin egg noodles

For the sauce
2 tablespoons peanut oil
1 pound ground pork or turkey
2 tablespoons brown bean sauce
1 tablespoon sugar
1 bunch green onions, minced
1 tablespoon ginger, minced
3 to 4 drops sesame oil

Step by Step

Make sure a grown-up has looked over the recipe and can help at the stove, especially with the stir-frying.

❖ Gather all ingredients and tools.
❖ First, cook the noodles. Fill the cooking pot half way with unsalted water and bring to a boil. Add the noodles. After the water returns to a boil, cook for 2 to 4 minutes. Carefully remove the pan from the stove and strain. Rinse noodles with cold water. Put in a bowl and set aside.
❖ Wash the green onions and carefully chop onions and ginger into small pieces. Set aside.
❖ Next, have the grown-up assist with heating oil in a wok or skillet and stir-frying the ground pork or turkey about 3 minutes until it just turns brown in color. Add the ginger followed by the bean sauce and stir-fry some more—about 3 minutes. Then, add the sugar and cook 2 more minutes. Top with the onions and shake a few drops of sesame oil over the whole mixture.
❖ Place noodles in bowls and ladle meat sauce on top. (Serves four full portions).

Today women as well as men enter the Dragon Boat races although they usually have their own teams.

Dragon Boat Festival

Have you ever seen boats that look like dragons? They have a wide open mouth at the bow and a scaly tail at the stern. Along the waterways, lakes, and rivers of central and south China, huge boats—some up to 100 feet long—arrive on one of the hottest days of the year to challenge each other to race. It's said that the dragon boat races are held to remember the river search for Qu Yuan, an ancient patriot and poet who lived over 2,000 years ago. Dragons are protective, powerful, and full of good tidings, so the boat races are one way of spreading good luck.

After the races, everyone spends the rest of the day looking at martial arts demonstrations, watching street theater or snacking on sweet buns, dragon-boat dumplings, and roasted pine nuts. Shop owners and children set off firecrackers long into the night. The day of the "double 5th" (5th Day of the 5th Month) draws to a close and the cycle of seasons moves from the growth of winter and spring (*yang* seasons) to the quiet of summer and autumn (*yin* seasons).

Dragon: The word for dragon in Chinese is **long**. Chinese dragons are strong and powerful and are used as a symbol for spring rain and growth.

The Race

Each boat in a Dragon Boat race belongs to a different village or association. They're painted different colors—green, red, yellow, white, and black. In most places, the races take place in the early afternoon. The boats begin to line up, and someone on the crew of each boat beats the drum to set the pace for the paddlers. When the starting gun is fired, they're off! It's wet and wild—the waves crashing into the boats and spray flying from the oars soaking everyone. What a splash! The winners take home prize money and the heads and tails of the boats (which are removable) are put away in nearby temples and club halls until next year's race.

The Hungry River Dragon

The Dragon Boat Festival honors Qu Yuan, China's earliest known poet. He served as a loyal minister to the king, but no one would listen to his advice on how to keep peace, and he was told to leave the kingdom forever. He became very sad and wrote a beautiful poem about his life and hopes while walking along the riverbank. That's the last anyone ever saw of him.

The people got into their boats to look for him in the river. They never found him, so they threw rice into the water for his soul to eat. But Qu Yuan didn't always have a chance to eat these offerings. This is the story that tells why.

There once was a fisherman who went to the river every day to fish. Each time he cast out his net, he sprinkled a handful of rice over the water to feed the river spirits.

One day he went to the river and tossed out his offering of rice. But he didn't catch a single fish. Instead, he heard someone shout,

"I am hungry!"

The next day, he threw out a few extra handfuls of rice. He started to fish but was startled again by a voice saying, **"I am hungry!"**

The third day he took a whole bag of rice and before casting out his net, threw all the grain into the river. Then he heard the voice again, only louder still, **"I am hungry!"** Suddenly, in full daylight, he caught sight of a man who called himself the poet Qu Yuan.

"What's wrong?" the fisherman cried, "Aren't you getting enough rice?"

"No!" Qu Yuan said. "A hungry dragon is eating all the rice. He has the eyes of a rabbit, the scales of a carp, the claws of a hawk, and the horns of a deer.

His voice is like the clanging of pots and pans, and when he's not eating he plays with a bright, gleaming pearl in the middle of his mouth. He's always following me around, and he's really quite a pest."

"What can I do?" the fisherman asked.

"Seal the rice with bamboo leaves and tie it together with different colored threads—green, red, yellow, white, and black." Qu Yuan instructed. "The colors will scare the dragon away."

The fisherman did as he was told, and sure enough the waters were still once more. He never heard from the soul of Qu Yuan again. And lucky for the fisherman, his nets were always full.

Today dumplings made from glutinous (sticky) rice are wrapped in leaves and tied with colored cords. They are eaten on the day of the Dragon Boat Festival to honor Qu Yuan. Little children also wear bracelets of five different colors as protection. After all, would you want a river dragon nibbling snacks out of your hand?

Five Poison Charm

In traditional China, people wore "five poison" (wu du) charms on the day of the Dragon Boat Festival. Five poisonous creatures—the snake, centipede, scorpion, lizard and frog (or sometimes a spider)—protected them against summertime diseases and danger. Nowadays, the five poison designs are used to decorate all sorts of things like clothing, quilts, and book bags. They are embroidered with bright colors and interesting patterns—you can find blue-striped snakes, pink lizards, or open-mouth frogs.

There are many kinds of sticky rice dumplings, each with its own special flavor, shape and type of leaf for wrapping. In South China lotus or bamboo leaves are used.

Dragon Boat Dumplings

Ingredients & Utensils

baking pan
sauce pan
mixing bowl
measuring cups and spoons
string—cotton twine
wok or big pot with lid
steamer
tongs

For the dumplings
2 cups glutinous rice flour
1/2 cup sugar
1/2 cup boiling water
2 tablespoons cold water
1 teaspoon banana extract
12 dried bamboo or cast iron leaves (available at Chinese groceries in neatly tied bundles)
vegetable oil for brushing leaves

For the sweet filling
1 cup canned sweetened red bean paste or melon seed or lotus seed paste. (A sweet, thick, firm paste made from mashed red beans.)

Step by Step

Make sure a grown-up has looked over the recipe and can help at the stove.

- ❖ Gather all ingredients and tools. Soak leaves in a pan of warm water until soft (1 hour for cast iron, 4 hours for bamboo).
- ❖ Put the rice flour in the mixing bowl. Bring to a boil in a sauce pan: 1/2 cup sugar in 1/2 cup of water. Add extract to liquid. Pour into flour, add 2 tablespoons of cold water, and mix with a fork into a squeezable dough. Knead (knuckling and punching) until smooth. Put it on a lightly floured clean surface and using your hands, roll out into a sausage shape. Cut into 12 pieces and roll each into a ball.
- ❖ Pat the leaves dry and brush with oil. Flatten the dough balls with your hands. Place a tablespoon of the paste into the center of the dough and wrap the dough around the filling, bringing up the edges to seal.
- ❖ Place near the corner end of a leaf and wrap the leaf around it so that nothing falls out. A four–sided shape looks nice. Tie with string.
- ❖ Steam the dumplings in a covered steamer for 15 to 20 minutes. Carefully take them out with tongs. Unwrap and eat (not the leaves!). Serve hot or cold. (Makes 12 tasty treats).

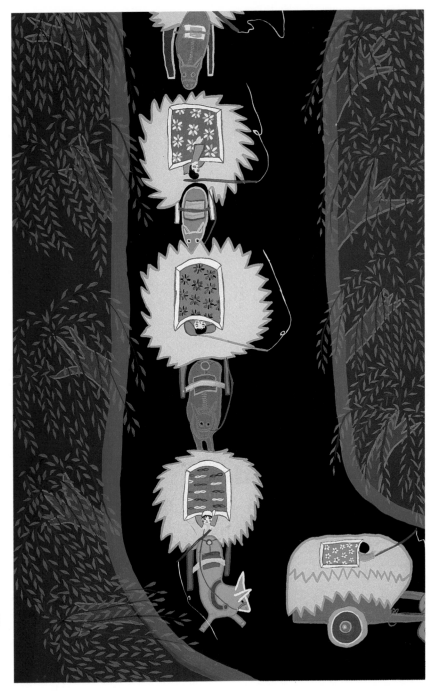

China's farmers grow the food for over one billion people. A good grain harvest has always been something to celebrate.

Moon Festival

Secret wishes are saved for the night of the Moon Festival. It is celebrated around mid-September—on the 15th Day of the 8th Lunar Month, exactly in the middle of the autumn season. In North China, crops of wheat have been gathered and in South China rice has been harvested. As for the moon, it looks bigger, brighter, and closer to earth at this time of year than at any other. Children like to ride along when the grain is taken to market. As day turns into night, they look up at the silver face of the moon and imagine all kinds of moon creatures until they fall asleep.

Sometimes at home they might take a mattress out in the yard, lie on it, and gaze at the moon. But it's not a time to be alone. Friends and relatives who live far away like to get together for picnics. They bring boxes of mooncakes to eat and everyone tells stories late into the night in honor of the Moon Lady, Chang E. This is a special time, when the Moon Lady grants wishes to those who send her their one-of-a-kind, unforgettable, never-heard-by-anyone requests.

Moon: Called **yue** in Chinese, the moon is a dark yin place; the sun a warm yang place.

41

Chang E Flies to the Moon

At the marketplace during the Moon Festival, there are shadow puppet plays and operas about how Chang E flew to the moon and became the Goddess of the Palace of Great Cold.

Big sisters, mothers and grandmothers buy all kinds of round fruits—crab apples, grapes, honey peaches, and pomegranates—so they can prepare special plates in honor of Chang E. These plates are set up at nighttime in the courtyard. Chang E knows about love and secret wishes so girls like her most of all, but she is celebrated by everyone as the Moon Goddess, and this is how she came to be . . .

Long, long ago when you could pull the tail of a tiger or walk on a snake, there were ten suns blazing in the sky. A man saved the world from burning by shooting down nine of the suns with his bow and arrows. As a reward, the Queen Mother of the West gave this Master Archer a magic potion that would let him live forever. The Archer carefully hid the potion until he felt he was worthy enough to drink it.

One day while he was away, his wife Chang E noticed a mysterious glow coming from a corner of their house. She followed the beam of light, discovered the magic potion, and drank it. Just as she did this, the Archer arrived home and saw Chang E rising into the night sky.

"Wait! Do not leave!" he cried.

He started to chase after her, but she passed right by in front of him, looking about the size of a toad.

Chang E flew straight into the night until she reached the moon.

"Oh my! Such a still and silent place," she thought.

There were forests of cinnamon trees and dusty rocks everywhere.

Suddenly Chang E sneezed and coughed up the magic potion. It changed into a jade rabbit as misty white in color as the pale and silvery moon. The smiling rabbit hopped over to Chang E and began to prepare the secret recipe for long life with cloves from the cinnamon tree. All day long the rabbit kept Chang E company, humming and singing as he ground the magic ingredients. And he still does, right up to this very day!

As for the Archer, he took up living in the Palace of the Sun. But he missed Chang E, who now kept house in the Palace of the Moon. One lonely day he went to visit her and chopped down a grove of cinnamon trees to build the Palace of Great Cold. The inside rooms were the colors of the rainbow and the outside walls shimmered like silver crystals.

The Archer comes back to stay with Chang E in the Palace on the 15th day of every month when the moon is fullest. This is when people on earth most like to gaze at the moon. On the eighth month they send Chang E their most special wishes and the rabbit in the moon watches over their festive gatherings.

For a time, Chang E and the Archer are the happiest beings in the sky, but then the Bird of Dawn shakes the starlit night with its cry. It is time for the Archer and Chang E to part.

"Good-bye, Archer," Chang E waves.

"Good-bye, Chang E," the Archer replies as he flies back to the glowing sun.

The rabbit in the moon watches over the excitement in this village. What do you think about when you look at the full moon?

The Disappearing Mooncake

Once upon a time, two brothers lived in a small village. They were very excited because it was the Moon Festival and their mother had just given them each a mooncake to eat. Older Brother ate his in a hurry, but Younger Brother had not yet taken a bite out of his cake.

"Would you like me to make your mooncake look more like the moon?" offered Older Brother.

"Oh, that would be very nice. Can you really do that?" Younger Brother eagerly asked.

Without hesitating the least bit, the older boy took a bite of the mooncake that made it look just like a crescent moon. The little boy started to cry.

"Wait! You don't think this looks good? I can do better—let me give you a half moon!"

Older Brother then nibbled off the corners of the crescent so it now had a smooth edge. He presented the half-eaten cake to his little brother.

"But it's half gone!" moaned Younger Brother who was now becoming very hungry.

So Older Brother calmed him down by describing all the phases of the moon—the waxing half moon, the full moon, the waning half moon, and lastly, the new moon.

"This is when the moon's dark side is pointed toward the earth and can't be seen by anyone," he explained.

With that, he gulped the remainder of the cake, raised his hands upward in celebration of the new moon, and skipped away!

Each of the five colors stands for one of the Five Elements (green = wood, red = fire, yellow = earth, white = metal, and black = water). The Five Elements have been used since ancient times to describe how things work together in a cycle from beginning to end. It's like a game—wood can beat earth, but metal can pound wood; fire can melt metal, but water can put out fire; earth fills up the water, but—back to the beginning again—wood can beat earth. The cycle never ends. The Five Colors (and other sets of five like the five tastes, the five directions, and so on) are all tied to the cycle of Five Elements. They are symbols for the process of creation and were thought of as powerful charms for keeping all things in order.

Mooncakes

Mooncakes are round like the moon. The round shape is a symbol for togetherness and harmony. Made of flaked pastry, they often have egg yolks in the center (to represent the moon) and sweet fillings of red bean paste, lotus seed paste, or coconut. Mooncakes are stamped with designs of the Moon Lady, the Jade Rabbit, a three-legged toad, or groves of cinnamon trees.

In Chinese history, mooncakes were used to pass around secret messages. In the 14th century, mooncakes were used to tell people the time and place for the revolution against the foreign Mongols. Today people still put printed pieces of paper on mooncakes. You will always find a square piece of paper either attached to the bottom of a cake or pasted on top of the cake box.

Most people buy mooncakes rather than going to the trouble of making them at home. They are on sale in August of each year in Chinese communities everywhere. It is fun to join the crowd buying mooncakes of many different flavors.

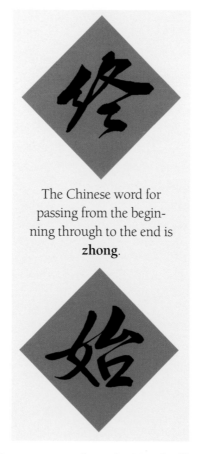

The Chinese word for
passing from the begin-
ning through to the end is
zhong.

The cycle of seasons is now complete. In North China the snows of winter settle over the earth. It's time for ice-skating, wearing padded coats, and buying snacks of sweet potatoes roasted over charcoal. In the warm South, the rains fill the waiting rice paddies. As the winter solstice passes, lengthening days pull the first green shoots from the vegetable fields. Stacks of bright oranges fill the markets, ready to greet the coming holiday crowds. As the cycle ends, it begins again, bringing another New Year and another promise of good fortune and happiness.

About the Paintings

The full-page color illustrations of festivals and daily life are by Chinese folk artists from two very different areas of China—Jinshan County southwest of Shanghai, and the towns of Wangxia and Xinji, almost 600 miles northwest in Hebei Province. Jinshan, in the wetlands of the South, is a rich farming area with many streams, canals, and waterway villages. Paintings from Jinshan reflect the traditional way of living based on wet-rice agriculture and fisheries. Wangxia and Xinji, in the dry landscape of the North, cope with extremes of climate. Paintings by these artists describe a life revolving around the planting of wheat and corn. Compared to the display of tropical colors, flowing rivers, and green hills of southern painting, there is a greater use of bold shapes and wintery scenes in folk painting from the North.

The artists range from 18-year-old teenagers to 80-year-old grandmothers. Most are amateurs who paint part-time and work in painting associations or cooperatives. In recent years, peasants, fisher people, herdsman, and workers throughout China have been encouraged to utilize their traditional artistic skills in new ways to describe the patterns and rhythms of agricultural life. The technique of easel painting is a new art form for these amateur artists. The content, however, derives from a long and rich tradition of folk art—embroidery, paper cutting, textile weaving, and woodblock printing. In a bold and whimsical style with patterned repetition that reflects the designs of rural life—rows of trees, fields of rice, flocks of geese—the artists paint the life around them, scenes based on everyday happenings and the harvest cycle. There are images of fireworks and lantern parades, planting and reaping, birthdays and weddings. Each picture is an individual expression of local life and culture, work and play. These paintings have been extensively exhibited in China and abroad and are currently gaining an enthusiastic response from viewers around the world.

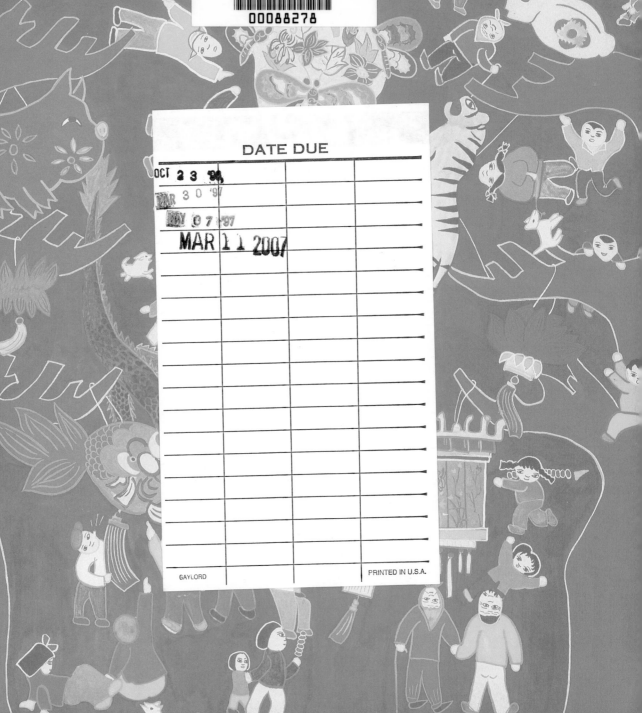